Even the Devil
is Afraid of a Shrew

A FOLKTALE OF LAPLAND Even the Devil

is Afraid of a Shrew

RETOLD BY VALERIE STALDER

ADAPTED BY RAY BROEKEL

ILLUSTRATED BY RICHARD BROWN

ADDISON-WESLEY

 AN ADDISONIAN PRESS BOOK

Printed in Japan.

Library of Congress Cataloging in Publication Data

Stalder, Valerie.
  Even the Devil is afraid of a shrew.

  SUMMARY: Recounts how a peaceful man got rid of
his nagging wife.
  "An Addisonian Press book."
  [1. Folklore—Lapland]   I. Brown, Richard,
1946-   illus. II. Title.
PZ8.1.S78Ev   398.21'09471'7   70-177415
ISBN 0-201-07188-6

In the very far north of Lapland
there once lived a man whose story is still told
and retold today–sometimes as a warning.
His name was Pava Jalvi.
And he was a peaceful, quiet man.

He had a wife who was very bad-tempered
and unpleasant—a real shrew.
She was always scolding and grumbling at him.
Nothing he ever did was right, poor man!
But everything his wife did was right,
according to her.

Now, one day in late summer,
when the cloudberries were ripe,
Pava Jalvi went out to pick some of them.
Cloudberries only grow in Lapland,
and are very delicious.

His wife stayed at home,
so he heard no grumbling voice.
Only the sweet voices of a few birds
kept him company.

Pava Jalvi looked all day.
But he did not find many cloudberries.
Towards evening, however, he came to a place
where there were more than he had seen all day.
They were all growing around the edge
of a deep hole in the ground.

The hole was so deep
that when Pava Jalvi looked down into it,
he could not see where it ended.
But it was getting late, so Pava Jalvi decided
to come back there again the next day.

When he got home,
his wife started to grumble at him again.
"Is this all you have found, you lazy,
good-for-nothing? You probably slept half the time
you were supposed to be looking!'
You never do anything right!"

Poor Pava Jalvi. He had done his best.
Then he remembered the cloudberries
around the deep hole.
So he told his wife about them.
He would go, he said, and get them the next day.
"Bah! You are no good
at finding berries," she sneered.
"But I am good at it—very good!
Tomorrow I shall go with you."

They both set out early the next morning.

But Pava Jalvi did not enjoy the day
as much as he had the one before.
Why? Because his wife never stopped
grumbling and complaining.
At last he began to feel angry.
And he wondered how he could
stop her terrible mouth.

When they got to the cloudberries
around the deep hole his wife shouted,
"Hurry up and pick them, you lazy-good-for-nothing!"

Suddenly Pava Jalvi felt very angry indeed.

He just had to do something to make his wife shut up.

So he pushed her over the edge of the hole!

Down, down, down she went.

Then down, down still further.

Pava Jalvi heaved a sigh of relief
at the peaceful silence.
For a long time afterwards he was happy.
But after a while, he began to feel rather lonely.
"Perhaps my wife has been
in that hole long enough," he said to himself.
"Maybe she has stopped grumbling by now.
I think I'll try to get her back up again."
Yes, but how?
He thought about the problem for some time.
Then he got the idea of tying together
some strong plants to make a long rope.

At the end he tied a stone.

Then he tossed the plant-rope into the hole.

But the rope was not long enough

to touch the bottom.

So Pava Jalvi pulled it up.

He tied more plants to it.

Then he tried again, and again, and again.

But it was still too short.

However, Pava Jalvi was a very,

very patient man. And one day,

three years after he had first started his plant-rope,

he at last felt it touch the bottom.

And, less than half a minute later,

he felt a weight as someone jumped

on the end of the rope.

"Ah, that must be my wife!"

he thought to himself.

So he began to pull the rope up again,

as fast as he could.

He pulled–and pulled–and PULLED–
until at last a face appeared at the edge of the hole,
and its owner scrambled out beside him.
But it was not his wife!!
No, it was THE DEVIL!
And very hot and bothered
the Devil looked, too.
Even for someone with his reputation!
"Thank you–thank you!" he gasped
to the startled Pava Jalvi.
"I thought I would *never* escape
from that terrible woman!"
"M-my w-wife?" stuttered Pava Jalvi.
"W-where is she? Why didn't *she* jump
on my plant-rope?"
"Oh–she tried to!" the Devil said,
"but I was desperate! I pushed her away
and climbed the plant-rope instead!
Oh, what a dreadful time she has given me–
ever since the day she first arrived!
She has made my life utter hell!"

The devil continued, "I am so grateful to you
that I will reward you well for rescuing me!
Here. Take my purse. It contains many gold pieces.
Enough to make you a very rich man."

And then the Devil rushed off.
Probably to make trouble for people.
And that is just what he did.
The Devil began to cause all kinds of trouble
for the people of the town.

And poor Pava Jalvi knew it was all his fault.

He had made the plant-rope, and the Devil had climbed
up the plant-rope out of the hole.

But Pava Jalvi was a patient man.

He thought and thought how he might get rid of the Devil.

Then he had an idea, and started walking
to the nearby fort.

In the fort were twelve cannons.
And a soldier took care of them.
To this soldier Pava Jalvi gave forty gold pieces.
"Here is what I want you to do.
Shoot off all twelve cannons three times.
Just for that you can keep all the money."
And the soldier shot off the cannons three times,
as Pava Jalvi wished.

Now as Pava Jalvi walked back to his house,

who should appear but the Devil.

"I am really enjoying myself," the Devil shouted.

"Making trouble for people is fun."

To which Pava Jalvi replied,

"I am glad you are here,

because I have been looking for you.

I want to WARN YOU!"

"Warn me? What about?" asked the Devil.

"Didn't you hear that loud noise
which boomed three times?
That was my wife—
she has climbed out of the hole—
and she is looking for you."
That was enough for the Devil!
WHOOSH!
He couldn't run fast enough!
And as he ran, he thought to himself,
"If that terrible woman has climbed
out of the hole—then the safest place
for me is down inside it!

But I must block the entrance after me."
So the Devil balanced a heavy stone
across the hole. He pushed and struggled
to get it into position.
Then he crept underneath it—and moved it
across the top so the hole was completely blocked.
He went down-down-down, and then down-down-down
still further.

It served him right that he found Pava Jalvi's
shrewish wife still there when he got to the bottom!
And unless someone has let them out
through another hole—they are both there yet.

And Pava Jalvi?

He still picked cloudberries.

And listened to the sweet voices of birds.

After all, he was a peaceful and quiet man.

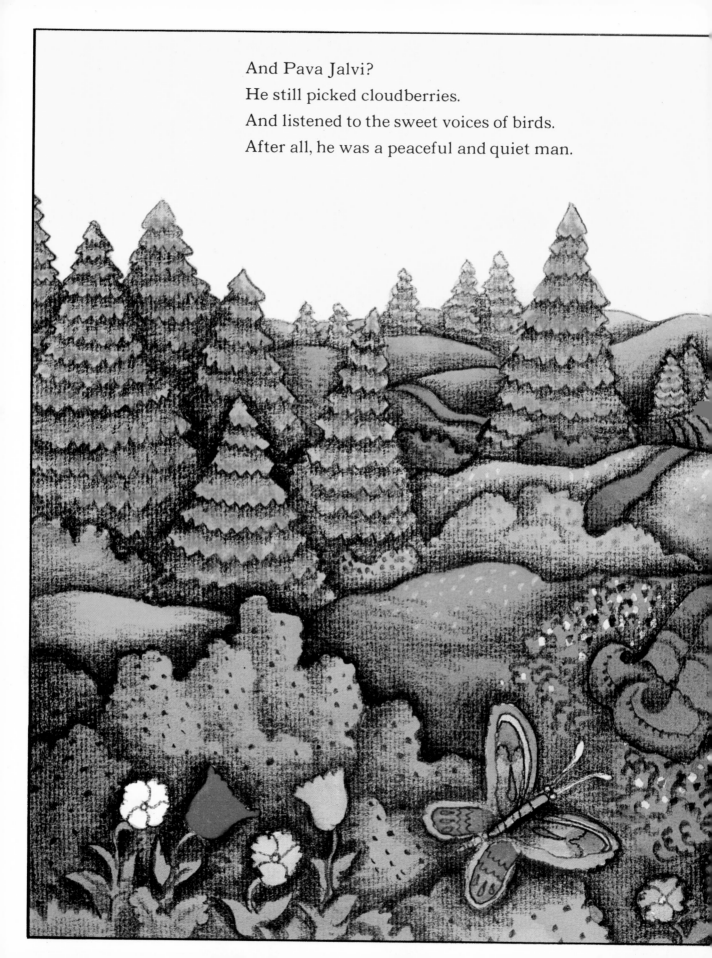